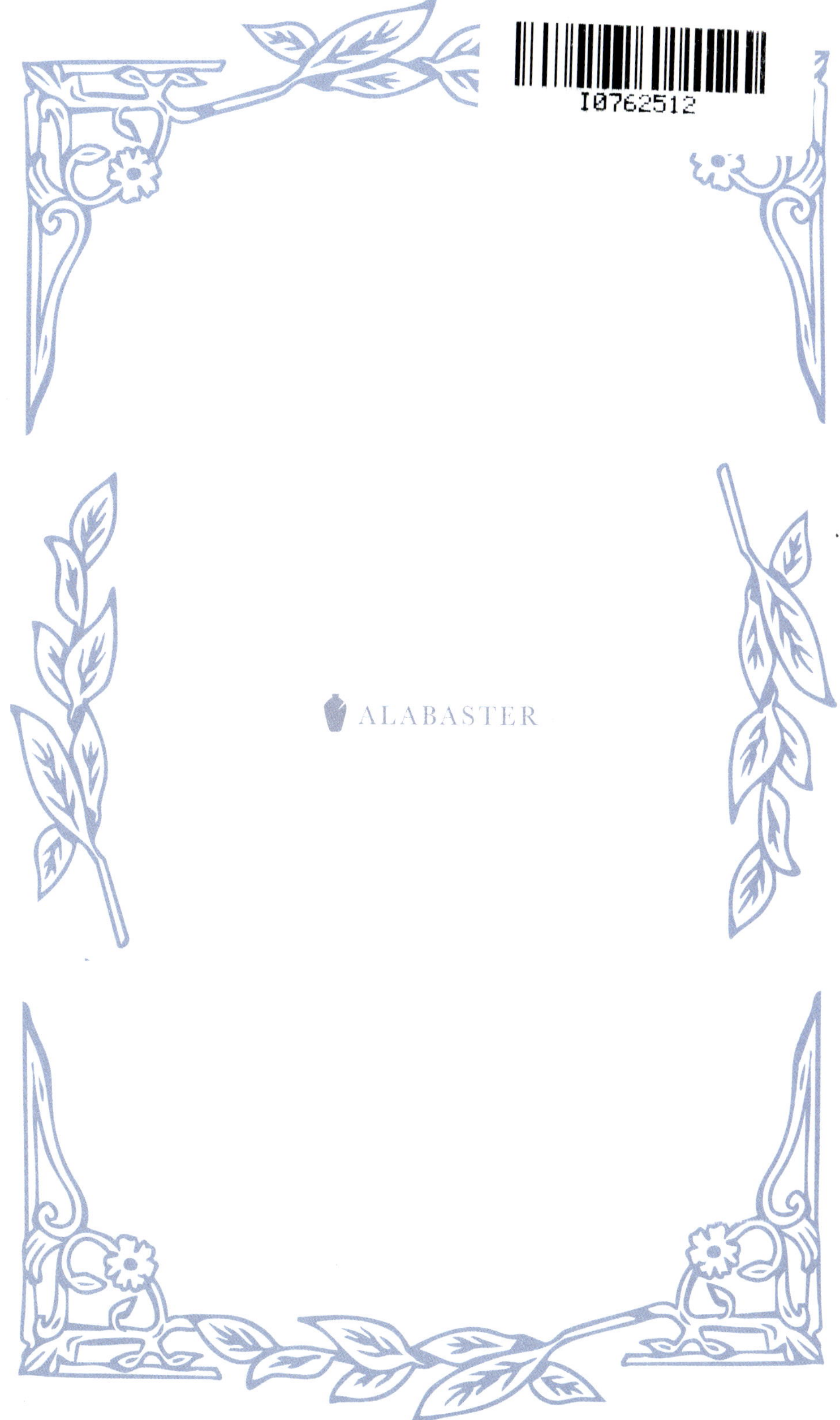
ALABASTER

Published in Los Angeles by Alabaster Creative Inc.

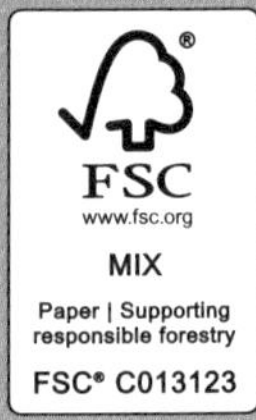

Printed in Italy by Graphicom S.r.l.

Contact
hello@alabasterco.com
www.alabasterco.com

Alabaster Co explores the intersection of creativity, beauty, and faith. Founded in 2016. Based in Los Angeles.

MY DAD'S

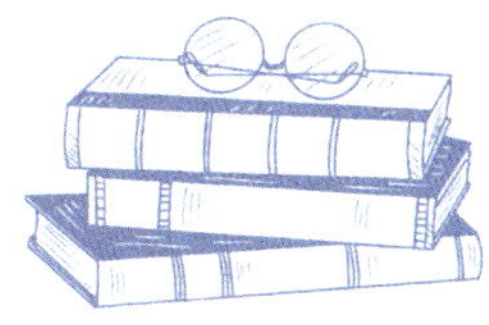

TESTIMONY

TABLE OF CONTENTS

> "If God's plan really is to make his invisible grace visible by sending parents of grace to give grace to children who desperately need grace, then I am called not just to preach that grace but to live and model it for my children every day."
>
> PAUL DAVID TRIPP

Each of us is a work in progress. As we navigate the highs and lows of life, we grow and change in accordance with our experiences. But, caught up as we are in the day-to-day, it can be difficult to step back and reflect on our stories, to recognize those defining and stretching moments. Without that intentional reflection, sharing the wisdom of our experience with others is even more daunting. Where do we begin? How can we meaningfully convey the histories of our lives to one who wasn't there for it all?

Enter *My Dad's Testimony*, an interactive journal to guide fathers in sharing their walks with God in their own words. Parenthood is one of life's greatest journeys. As we help our children develop and grow, we too are transformed; our understanding of the world and our faith deepens and expands. These are the lessons that scripture urges us to share: "He commanded our ancestors to teach them to their children, so the next generation might know them—even the children not yet born—and they, in turn, will teach their own children. So each generation should set its hope anew on God, not forgetting his glorious miracles and obeying his commands." (Psalm 78:5-7). This book is designed to help dads recount the wisdom—the delights and challenges—learned throughout the years and to explore the connection between the experiences of fatherhood and our relationship with our Heavenly Father.

Divided into six major sections, *My Dad's Testimony* provides thoughtful prompts to guide you in sharing your story. Whether you complete this journal collaboratively with your child(ren), talking through each question and prompt together, or independently to share as a keepsake in the future, remember that this exercise is, at its core, a conversation. It is an opportunity for different generations to come together, to learn and listen. Instead of serving as a formulaic interview, we hope these questions might start a dialogue between parent and child. At the end of each section, you will find a place for concluding prayers. Use this space to reflect on the experience of walking through the preceding questions. What has God taught you through that process? What are your hopes for those who, in the future, will read and reflect on the answers you gave?

May this journal help you and your child(ren) draw closer together. And may the reflections and conversations sparked here illuminate the bold and beautiful ways that God has been at work all the days of our lives. *Amen.*

01

EARLY FAITH

“THIS GOOD NEWS TELLS
US HOW GOD MAKES US
RIGHT IN HIS SIGHT. THIS IS
ACCOMPLISHED FROM START

TO FINISH BY FAITH.
AS THE SCRIPTURES SAY,
‘IT IS THROUGH FAITH THAT A
RIGHTEOUS PERSON HAS LIFE.”

ROMANS 1:17, NLT

When did you first come to faith?
Or, if you grew up in the Church, when did
your faith first become real to you?

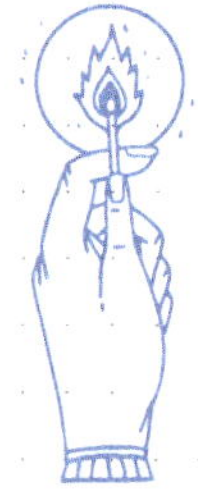

Was there a particular moment or experience that led you to explore faith more deeply?

Who introduced you to the Gospel and how did they come alongside you?

How did your faith in Jesus affect your relationships? Was it a source of commonality and togetherness? Or, did it result in any friction between you and your family and friends?

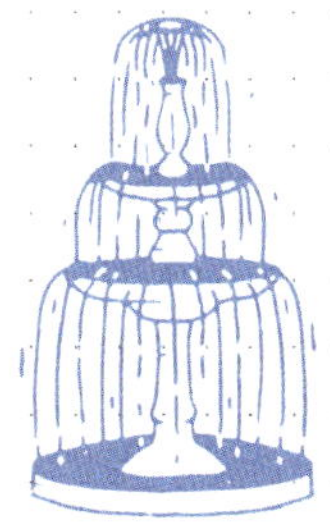

Were you a part of a church or faith community at this time? If so, what was that community like?

Looking back, how would you describe your relationship with Jesus in these early days of faith?

Were there any doubts or questions you had early on? How did you navigate them?

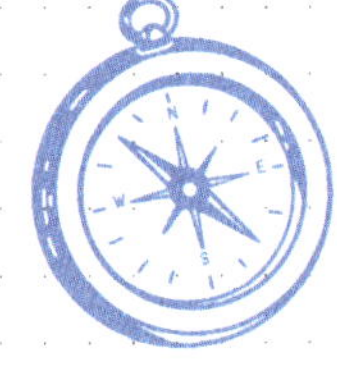

How did those around you help you wrestle with these questions? Were you encouraged to prayerfully reflect on your doubts, or was this discouraged?

Concluding Prayers

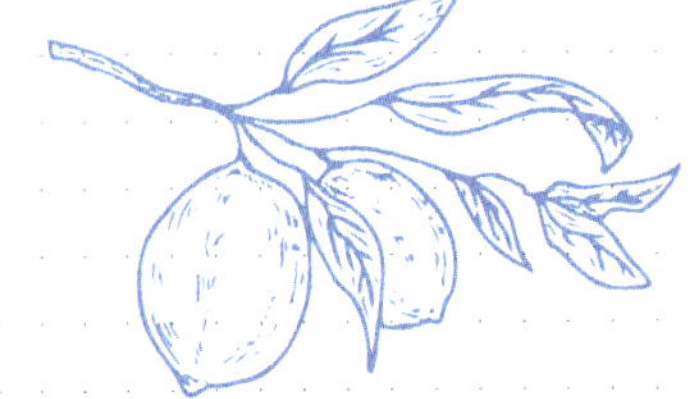

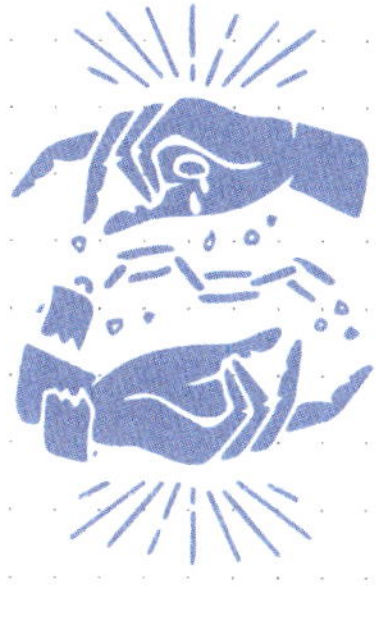

MY DAD'S TESTIMONY

“FOR THIS IS HOW GOD LOVED THE WORLD: HE GAVE HIS ONE AND ONLY SON, SO THAT EVERYONE WHO BELIEVES IN HIM WILL NOT PERISH BUT HAVE ETERNAL LIFE.”

JOHN 3:16, NLT

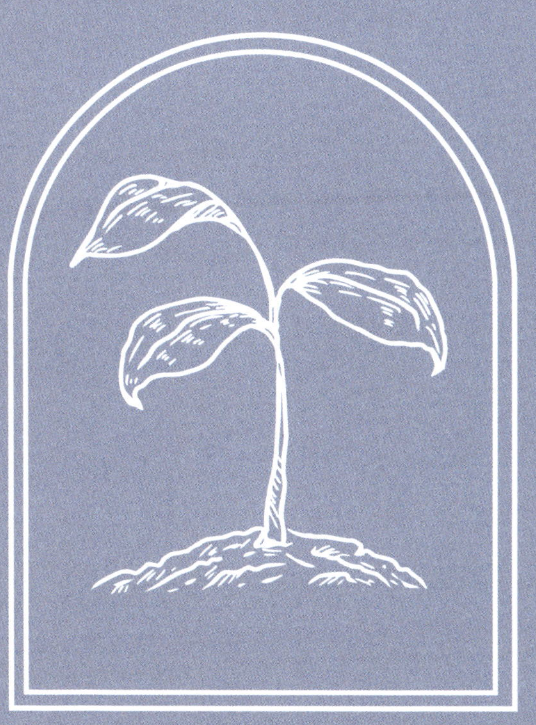

02

LIVING OUT FAITH

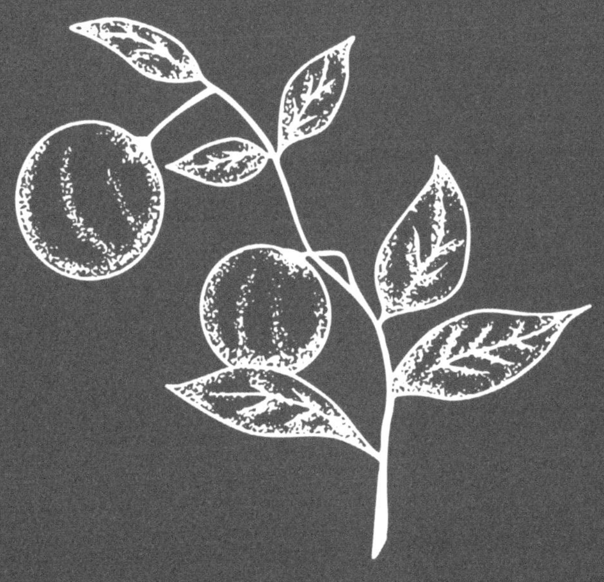

“THIS IS WHAT THE PAST IS FOR! EVERY EXPERIENCE GOD GIVES US, EVERY PERSON HE PUTS IN OUR

LIVES IS THE PERFECT PREPARATION FOR THE FUTURE THAT ONLY HE CAN SEE."

CORRIE TEN BOOM

How have your beliefs shaped the way you handle everyday challenges?

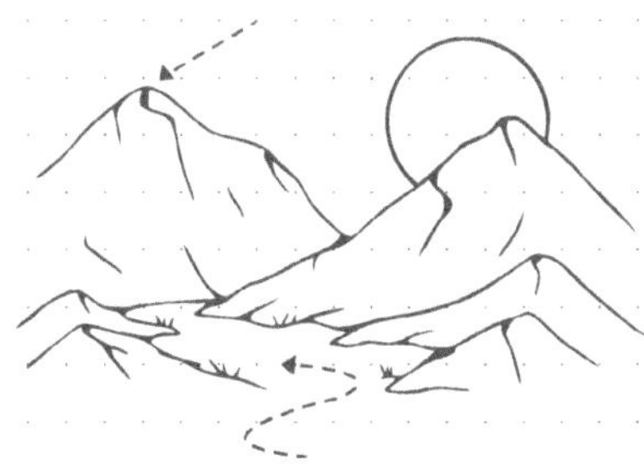

Can you think of a time when another person showed you radical love? What was that like, and how did it make you feel?

Likewise, describe a time when you showed radical love and/or kindness to another person. How did they respond? What did that moment teach you?

Have there been moments when living out your beliefs felt particularly difficult or went against the grain? How did you handle that?

In your experience, how do faith and community relate to one another?

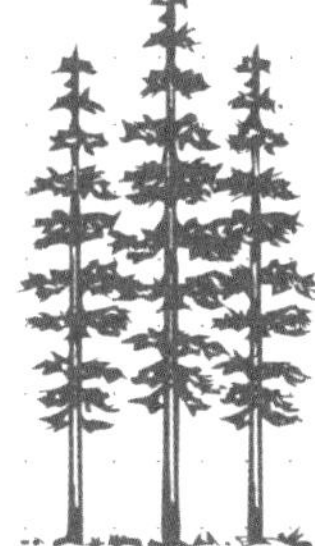

What does forgiveness mean to you? How have you experienced forgiveness from others? How have you extended it?

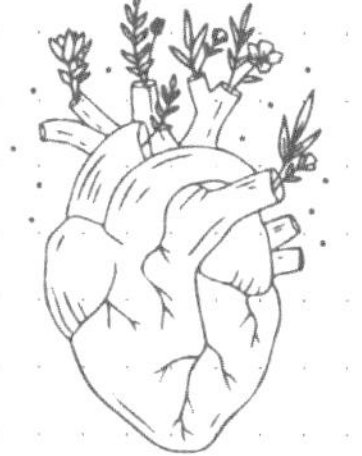

What makes you feel hopeful?
How do hope and faith intertwine
with one another in your life?

How do you engage with the practice of prayer? How has your prayer life developed over the years?

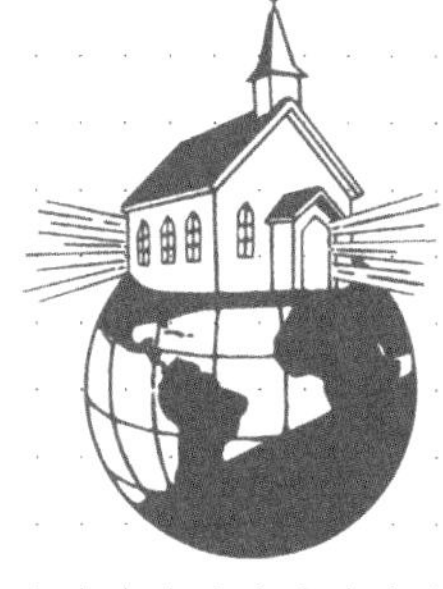

Concluding Prayers

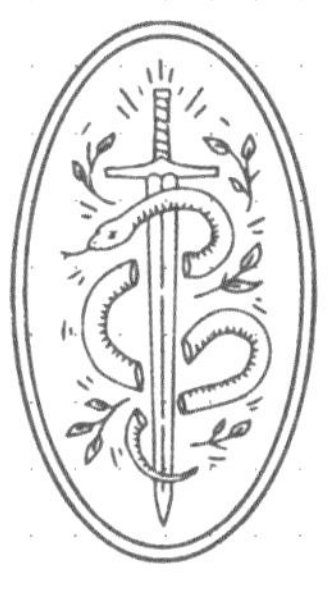

MY DAD'S TESTIMONY

"JESUS SPOKE TO THE PEOPLE ONCE MORE AND SAID, 'I AM THE LIGHT OF THE WORLD. IF YOU FOLLOW ME, YOU WON'T HAVE TO WALK IN DARKNESS, BECAUSE YOU WILL HAVE THE LIGHT THAT LEADS TO LIFE.'"

JOHN 8:12, NLT

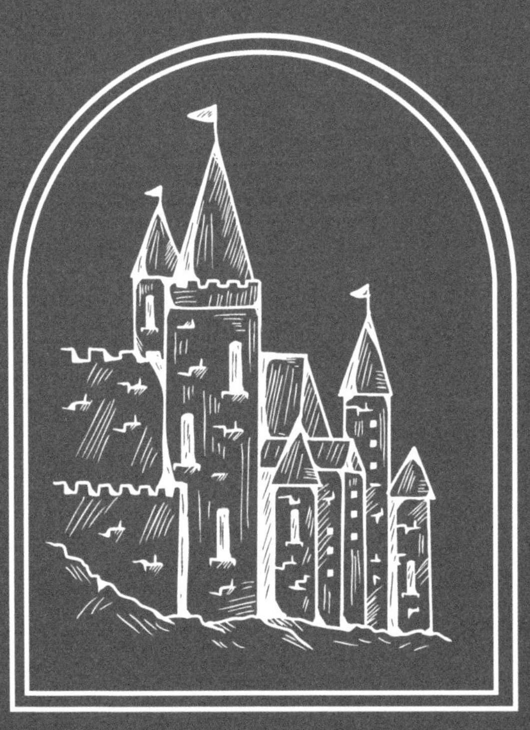

03

REFLECTING ON THE BIBLE

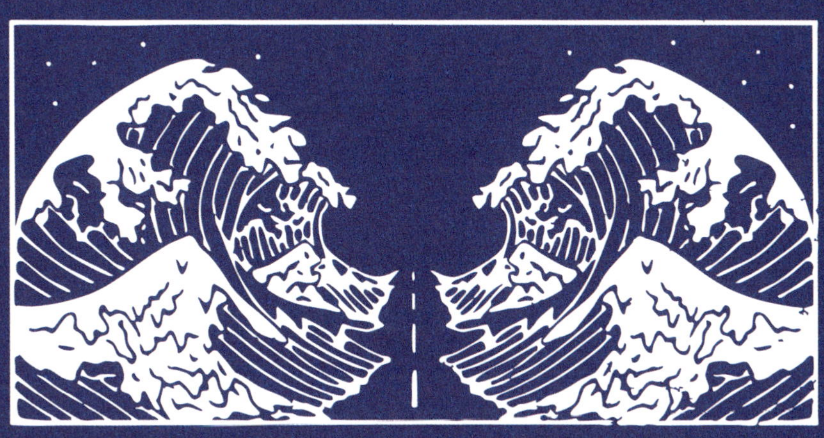

“WHEN I DISCOVERED YOUR WORDS, I DEVOURED THEM. THEY ARE MY JOY AND

MY HEART'S DELIGHT, FOR I BEAR YOUR NAME, O LORD GOD OF HEAVEN'S ARMIES."

JEREMIAH 15:16, NLT

What is your favorite book of the Bible? What makes it your favorite?

Is there a particular biblical figure you really relate to? What is it about that person's story that speaks to you?

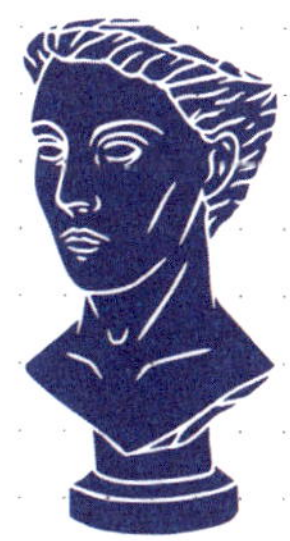

On the flip side, is there a figure from the Bible you struggle to understand? What makes them difficult for you to resonate with?

Is there a Bible passage through which you feel God truly spoke to you? What were the circumstances of that season of your life?

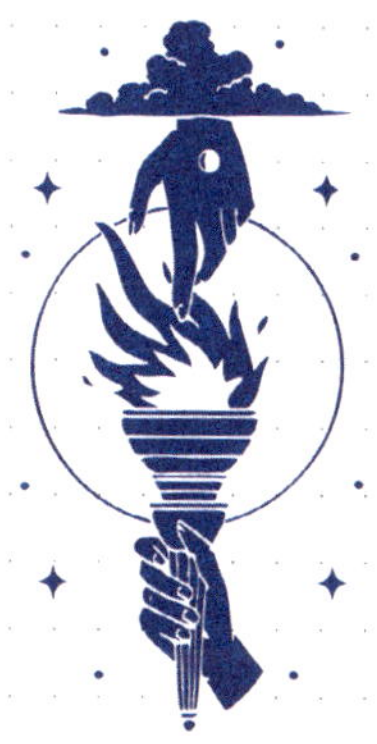

Do you have a life verse or favorite verse from scripture? If so, which one?

How do you approach reading the Bible—do you follow a specific method or practice?

What has the Bible taught you about fatherhood? How have you applied those lessons to your approach as a parent?

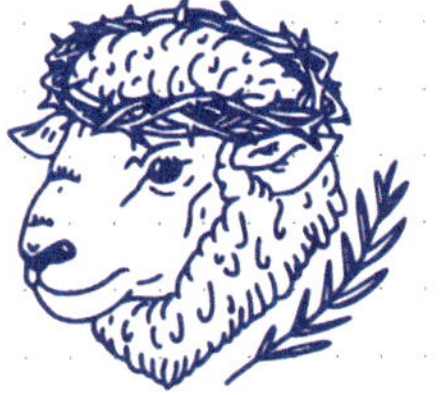

Do you have a preferred Bible translation? If so, what is it about that translation that you appreciate?

Concluding Prayers

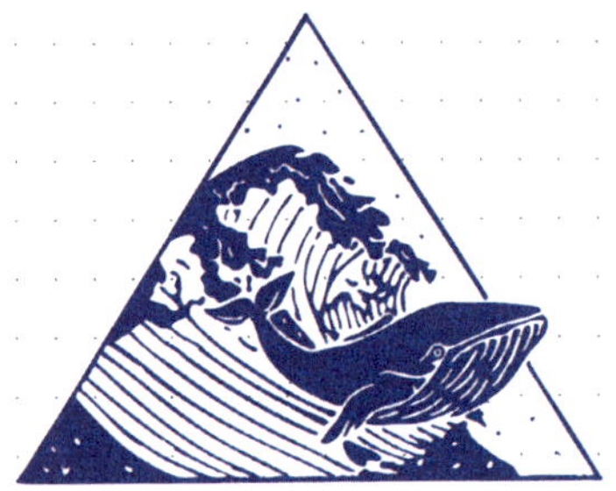

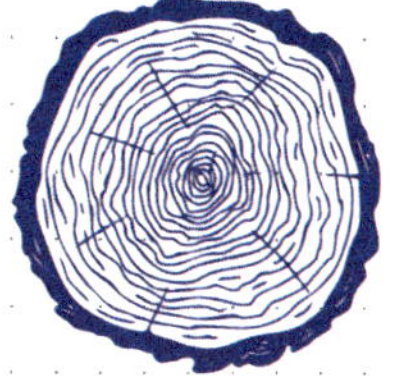

MY DAD'S TESTIMONY

“THE GRASS WITHERS
AND THE FLOWERS FADE,
BUT THE WORD OF OUR
GOD STANDS FOREVER.”

ISAIAH 40:8, NLT

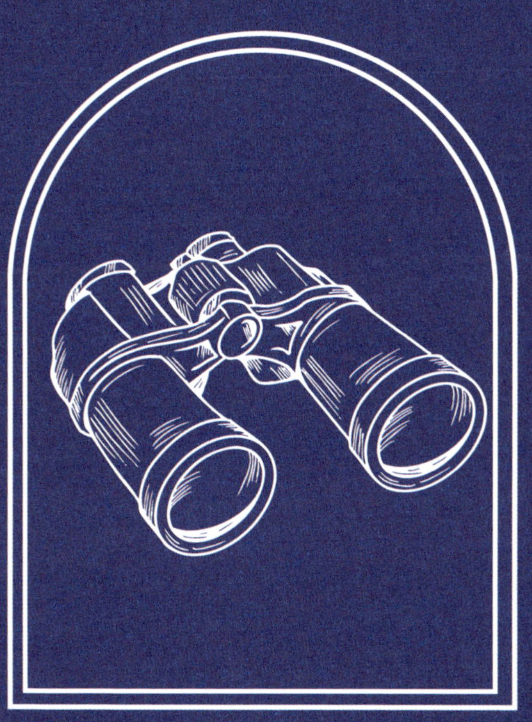

04

BECOMING A DAD

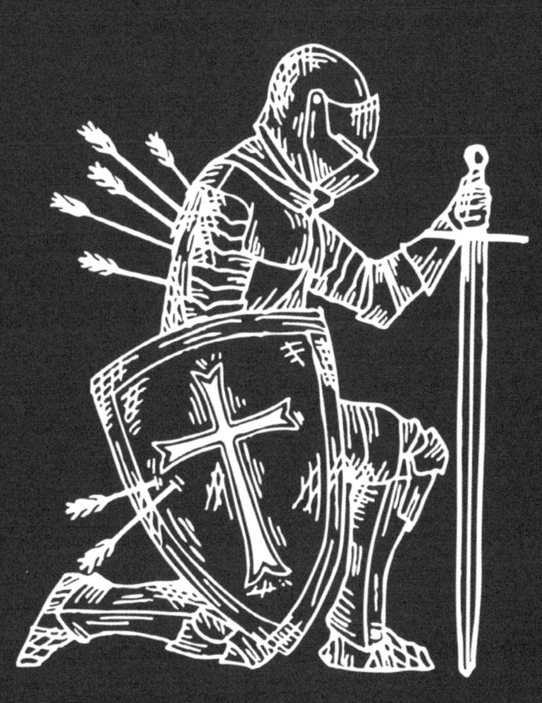

“LOVE IS AT THE
ROOT OF EVERYTHING.
ALL LEARNING,

ALL PARENTING,
ALL RELATIONSHIPS.
LOVE OR THE LACK OF IT."

FRED ROGERS

Share about the moment you
first learned you would be a father.
Were you excited? Nervous?

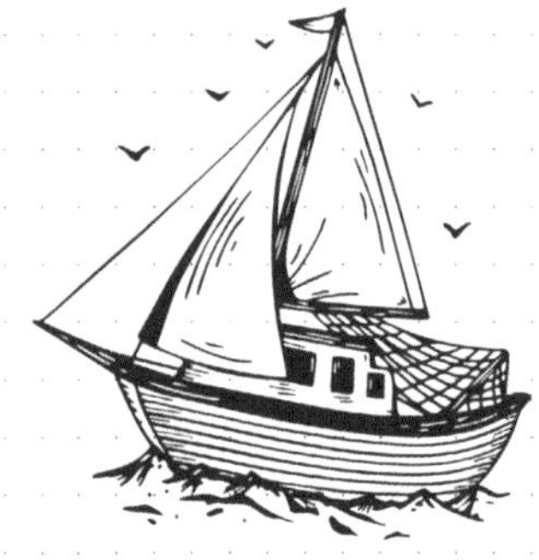

Were there any specific moments during those early days that stand out as particularly joyful or overwhelming?

Who did you look to for guidance or support as you entered fatherhood? Who were your role models?

Did your understanding of your faith change or evolve as you became a parent? How so?

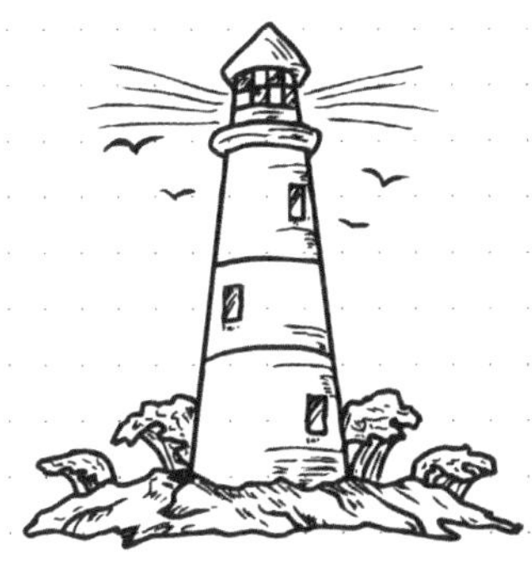

Do you recall any specific prayers you had for your child(ren) when they were first born?

How did you incorporate your faith into the way you nurtured and cared for your child(ren)?

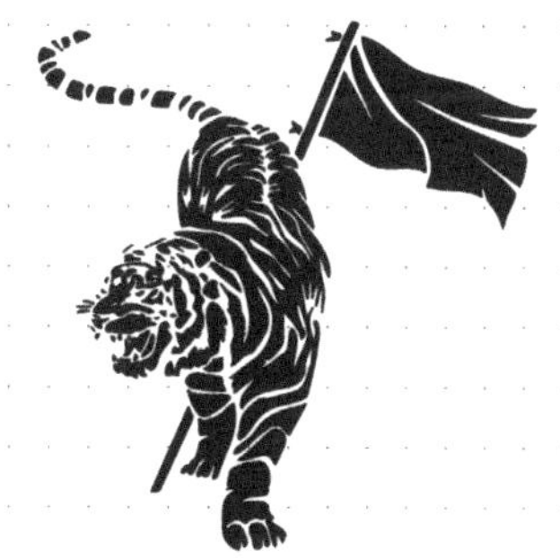

How did you choose your child(ren)'s name(s)? Was there a different name you almost chose instead?

Looking back, do you see any ways God was shaping or preparing you spiritually through the experience of early fatherhood?

Concluding Prayers

MY DAD'S TESTIMONY

"SHOW ME THE RIGHT PATH,
O LORD; POINT OUT THE ROAD
FOR ME TO FOLLOW. LEAD ME
BY YOUR TRUTH AND TEACH
ME, FOR YOU ARE THE GOD
WHO SAVES ME. ALL DAY
LONG I PUT MY HOPE IN YOU."

PSALM 25:4-5, NLT

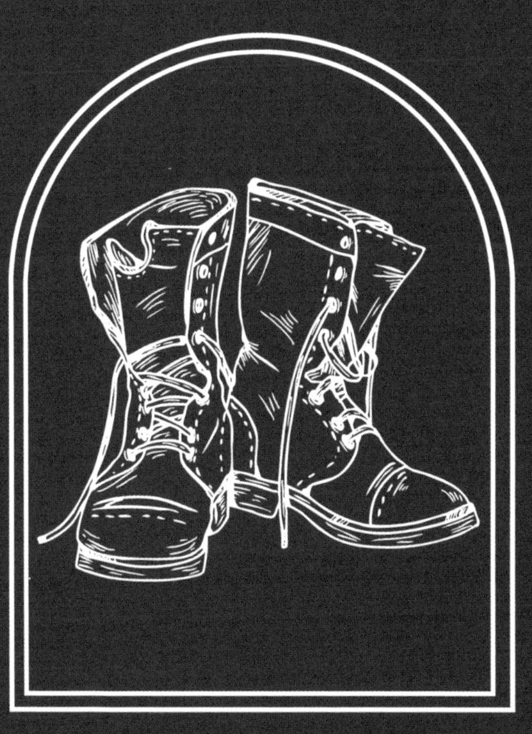

05

LESSONS THROUGHOUT FATHERHOOD

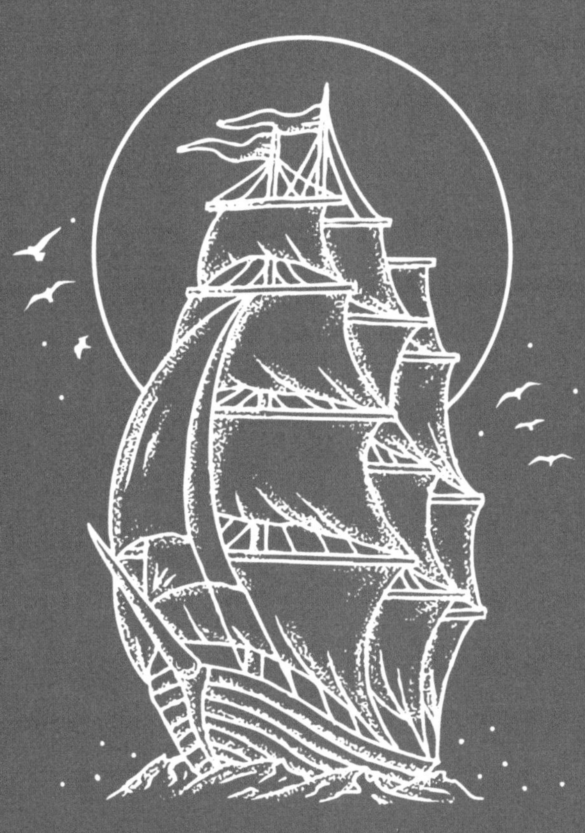

“THEN THE WAY YOU LIVE WILL ALWAYS HONOR AND PLEASE THE LORD, AND YOUR LIVES WILL PRODUCE EVERY

KIND OF GOOD FRUIT. ALL THE WHILE, YOU WILL GROW AS YOU LEARN TO KNOW GOD BETTER AND BETTER.”

COLOSSIANS 1:10, NLT

How has your understanding of fatherhood changed as your child(ren) grew older?

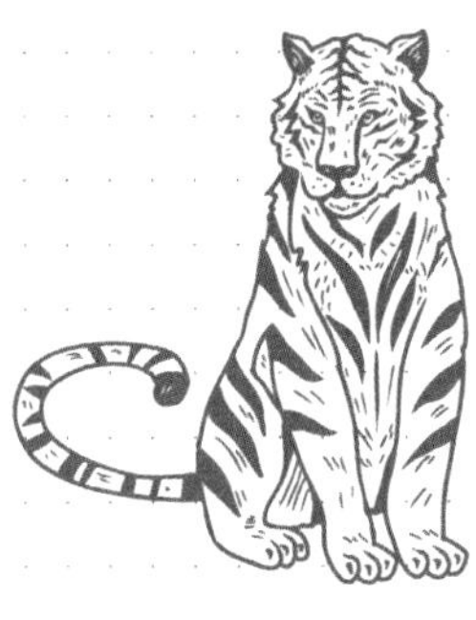

How did you foster a strong relationship with your child(ren), especially as they developed their own personalities?

How did you share your faith with your child(ren)? Did this approach change as they matured?

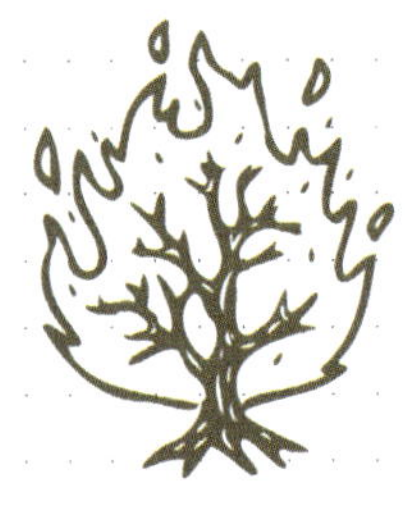

What is something *you* have learned from your kid(s)?

Looking back, what have been some of the most rewarding aspects of raising children, and what were the most challenging?

How did you navigate the tension between letting your child(ren) make their own choices and guiding them with your values?

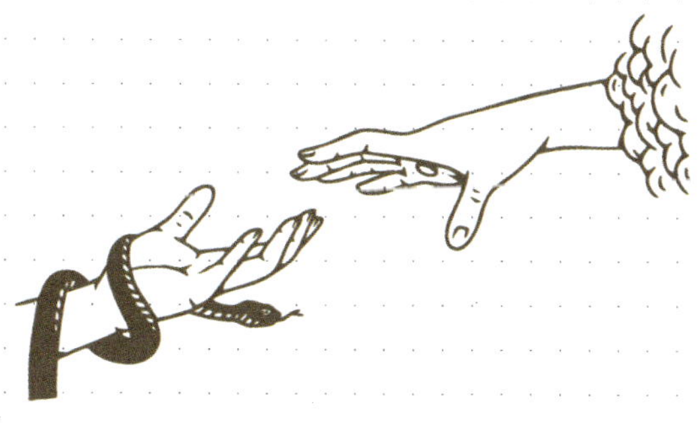

How have you seen God's presence or purpose in the growth and development of your child(ren)?

As you reflect on your journey as a father, how has your relationship with God deepened or changed over the years?

Concluding Prayers

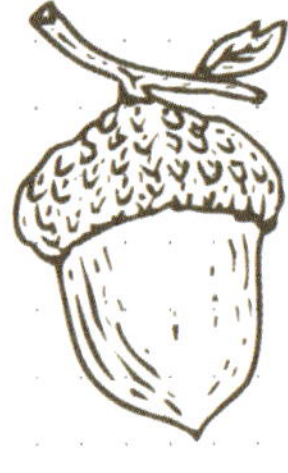

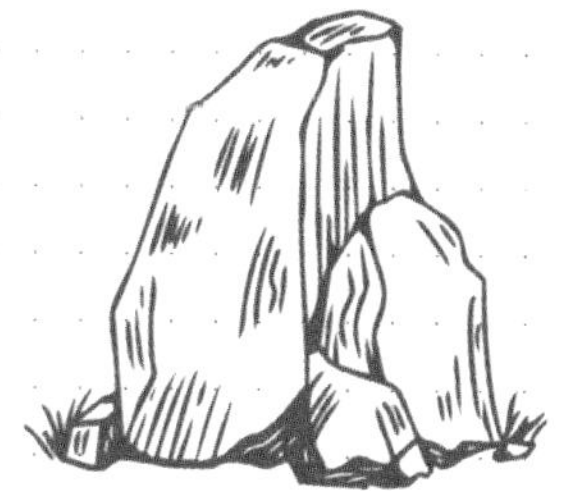

MY DAD'S TESTIMONY

"TEACH ME TO DO YOUR
WILL, FOR YOU ARE MY
GOD. MAY YOUR GRACIOUS
SPIRIT LEAD ME FORWARD
ON A FIRM FOOTING."

PSALM 143:10, NLT

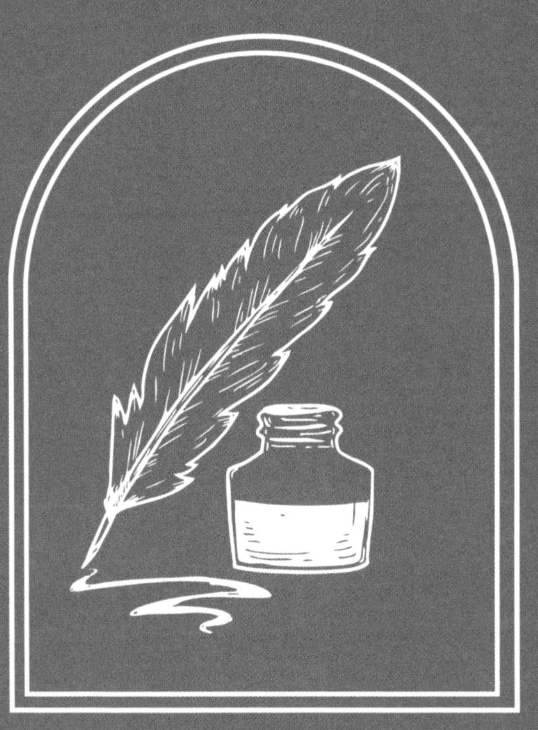

06

DAD'S FAVORITES

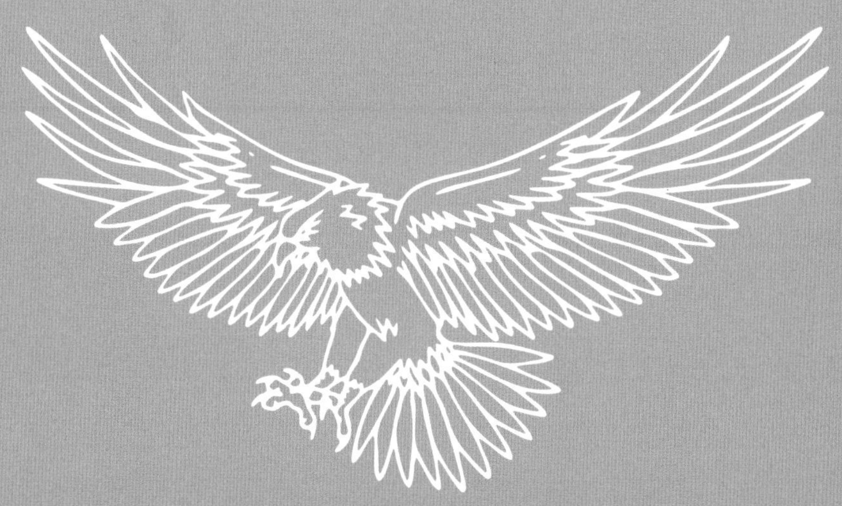

“LIFTING OUR CUP MEANS SHARING OUR LIFE SO WE CAN CELEBRATE IT. WHEN WE TRULY BELIEVE WE ARE CALLED TO LAY

DOWN OUR LIVES FOR OUR FRIENDS, WE MUST DARE TO TAKE THE RISK TO LET OTHERS KNOW WHAT WE ARE LIVING."

HENRI NOUWEN

If you were to make a list of books you think everyone should read, what books would be on the list? What is it about those books that made an impact on you?

What songs would make your "favorites" playlist? Why?

What's the best meal you've ever had? What about that experience particularly stands out to you?

What is your favorite pastime and what do you enjoy about it?

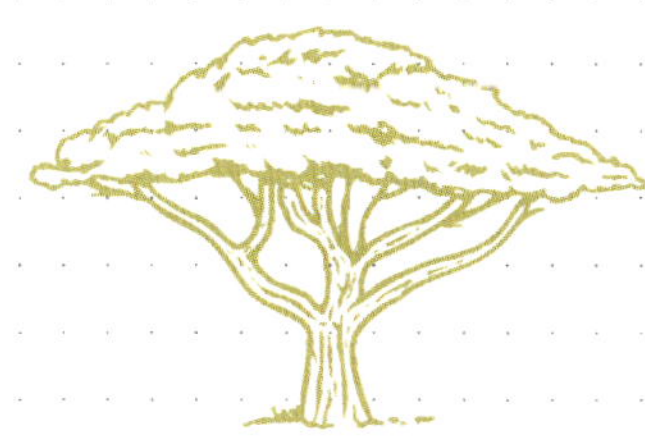

Is there a place or activity that makes you feel closest to God?

What does "strength" mean to you? What are your favorite examples of strength in action?

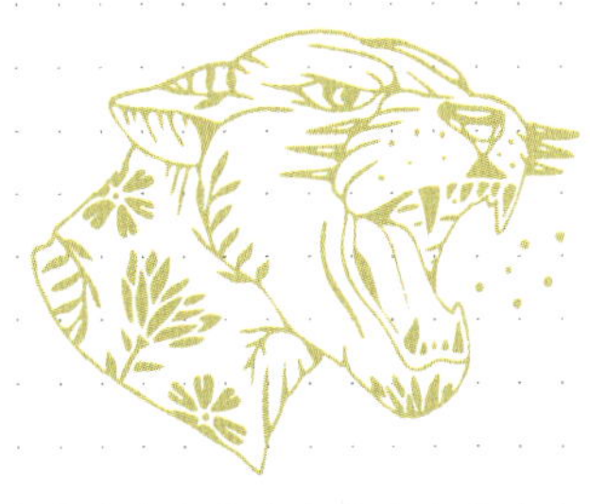

Who in your life has been a spiritual mentor to you? What have you learned from them, and how have they walked alongside you?

What public figures (past or present) have had the most influence on your life and your faith journey?

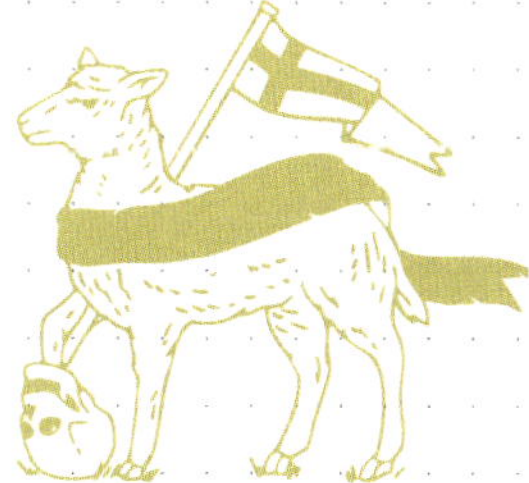

Concluding Prayers

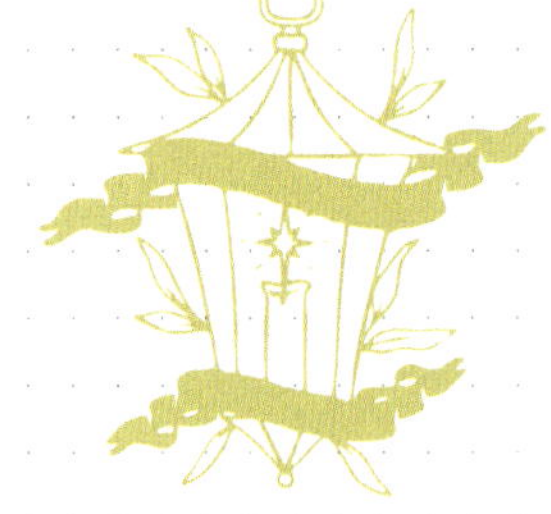

“YES, THE LORD POURS DOWN HIS BLESSINGS. OUR LAND WILL YIELD ITS BOUNTIFUL HARVEST.”

PSALM 85:12, NLT

Further Wisdom

Use this space to expand upon any of your answers, or to share further thoughts and advice.

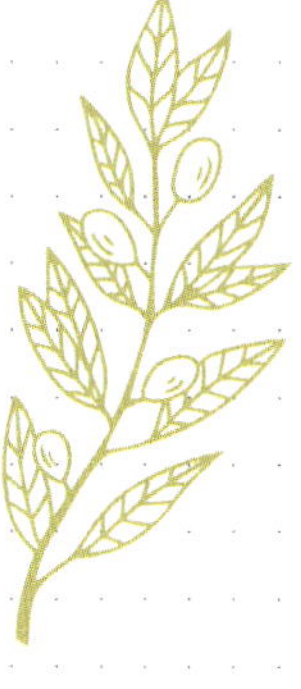

CREDITS

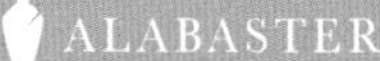

TEAM

COLLIN ELDRIDGE

CHRISTINA WOO

DANIEL HAN

ELLEN WEI

EMALY TWEITMANN

EMMA TWEITMANN

JOSH JANG

JOYCE TAN

MARIA MADDOCKS

MINZI BAE

SAMUEL HAN

TYLER ZAK

VALERIE HUI

WILLA JIN

ARTWORK BY

ANDREW LENNON

LAYOUT DESIGN BY

RACHEL CHANG